Introductions

Introductions

Poets Present Poets

Edited by Evan Jones

with an introduction by

David Staines

Fitzhenry & Whiteside

© 2001 Fitzhenry & Whiteside. Individual works are copyright of their respective authors, unless otherwise noted.

ALL RIGHTS RESERVED. No part of this book may be reproduced in any manner without the express written consent of the publisher, except in the case of brief excerpts in critical reviews and articles.
All inquiries should be addressed to:

Fitzhenry & Whiteside Limited
195 Allstate Parkway
Markham, Ontario L3R 4T8

www.fitzhenry.ca,
godwit@fitzhenry

Fitzhenry & Whiteside acknowledges with thanks the Canada Council for the Arts, the Government of Canada through its Book Publishing Industry Development Program, and the Ontario Arts Council for their support of our publishing program.

National Library of Canada Cataloguing in Publication Data

Main entry under title:

Introductions: poets present poets

ISBN 1-55041-627-8

1. Canadian poetry (English) – 21st century.* 2. Canadian poetry (English) – 21st century – History and criticism.* I. Jones, Evan, 1973- .

PS8293.I583 2001   C811'.608   C2001-930099-9
PR9195.7.I583 2001

Cover and textual design: Karen Petherick, Markham, Ontario
Cover Image: Gerald Ferguson, Fish and Door (1992). Enamel on canvas, painted wood. Collection of the Art Gallery of Nova Scotia (purchased with funds provided by Trimark Investment Management).

Acknowledgements	7	
Introduction	9	by David Staines
Marilyn Bowering	11	by P.K. Page
James Clarke	19	by Susan Musgrave
Carla Funk	28	by Lorna Crozier
Susan Holbrook	37	by Erin Mouré
Suzette Mayr	45	by George Elliott Clarke
rob mclennan	53	by John Newlove
George Murray	61	by Richard Outram
Elizabeth Philips	69	by Patrick Lane
Karen Solie	75	by Don McKay
Helen Tsiriotakis	83	by Robert Kroetsch
Sheila Waite	91	by Anne Michaels
George Whipple	97	by Margaret Avison
Carleton Wilson	105	by A.F. Moritz
Selected Publications	111	

Contents

Marilyn Bowering's "The Mind's Road to Love" and "About Your Name" reprinted with permission from *Human Bodies, New and Selected Poems 1987-1999* (Vancouver: Beach Holme, 1999).

James Clarke's "How to Bribe a Judge" reprinted from *The Ancient Pedigree of Plums* (Toronto: Exile Editions, 1999). "Silver Mercies", "The End of Something" and "A Young Offender" reprinted from *Silver Mercies* (Toronto: Exile Editions, 1997).

Carla Funk's "Messengers" reprinted with permission from *Blessing the Bones into Light* (Victoria: Coteau Books, 1999).

Selections from Susan Holbrook's "Grim" reprinted with permission from *misled* (Red Deer, Alberta: Red Deer Press, 1999).

rob mclennan's "barely moving, barely thinking," "milk," and "stones & ice: a translation," appeared previously as above/ground press broadsides. "the restoration of st peters" appeared previously as a greenboathouse press broadside.

George Murray's "The Lion Tamer's Embalming," "The Palmist's Elegy," "The Mountebank's Wake," "The Somnambulist's Burial," and "The Coroner's Autopsy" reprinted with permission from *Carousel: A Book of Second Thoughts* (Toronto: Exile Editions, 2000).

Elizabeth Philips' "Orange" is reprinted from *A Blue with Blood in it* (Victoria: Coteau Books, 2000). "Meditation On Chuang-tzu," and "On the Path of the Deer" are reprinted from *Beyond My Keeping* (Victoria: Coteau Books, 1995). Permission is donated by the publisher.

Helen Tsiriotakis' "Mnemosyne I & II," "Shadow Hand," and "Constantly Stirring" reprinted with permission from *A House of White Rooms* (Toronto: Coach House Books, 2000).

George Whipple's "Music," and "Christmas Eve", reprinted with permission from *Carousel* (Victoria: Ekstasis Editions, 1999).

Acknowledgements

Introductions: Poets Present Poets is a breath of fresh air, a unique enterprise that offers some of Canada's most respected poets presenting younger poets, who should become major poets of the future *and* of the present. Here are many of this country's most influential writers pausing to give some guidance to the literary landscape that now includes these younger writers. When P.K. Page, this country's finest poet, singles out the poetry of Marilyn Bowering, we can sense the affinity between these two writers. Page observes Bowering's "cadence and the arc of her imagination that overrode the obscurities—obscurities I now think to be the result of a lateral and passionate mind. A visionary mind." Could these words not be a commentary, too, on much that Page has written? I remain grateful for this pressure into rereading a gifted and challenging artist.

The same position might also be said of Margaret Avison's admiration for George Whipple, whom, I suspect, she does not know. "Christmas Eve", "A Hymn to God The Father", and "Easter Egg" reach into the stillness beyond words. Because of Avison's prodding, I read all of Whipple, inveterate explorer of the world for the mysteries beyond the surface, beyond the natural.

And George Elliott Clarke's choice of Suzette Mayr: she had already anchored his anthology, *Eyeing the North Star: Directions in African-Canadian Literature* (1997), as its youngest contributor. Here, in this new anthology, she is a fascinating poet who deserves to be read carefully and seriously.

These three senior poets find in their junior colleagues poets who reverberate with many of the same concerns,

Introduction

whose verse pulsates with similar rhythms. And this is the case for many of the younger poets in this book.

"Every strong poetry has its own distinctive flavour or tang, the combination of qualities that makes it unique," states Don McKay, and this observation does not refute my statements. Rather, these younger poets create their own distinctive styles, even when they share many interests of their senior colleagues. McKay's choice, Karen Solie, is a vivid realist who writes with metaphorical verve of so many things; I look forward immensely to her first book. And Helen Tsiriotakis, Robert Kroetsch's choice, is a major poet whose book I must now read.

I could go on and on. *Introductions* renews forcefully my commitment to Canadian poetry.

David Staines
Dean of Arts, University of Ottawa
and Editor of the Journal of Canadian Poetry

At first glance it may seem strange that I have chosen MARILYN BOWERING for this anthology. Surely, as an example of neglect, I could have chosen almost any poet in the country. Our culture makes orphans of poets. But given that, why Marilyn Bowering? She has, after all, won many prizes and, for her latest novel, *Visible Worlds*, she was short-listed for the prestigious Orange Prize. But for her poetry—thirteen books of it—she has had remarkably little critical attention.

As I search for reasons why, I review my own responses to her work beginning with her earliest poetry. Even when incomprehensible to me, it always caught my attention. There was something about her cadence and the arc of her imagination that overrode the obscurities—obscurities I now think to be the result of a lateral and passionate mind. A visionary mind.

A prolific and adventurous writer, Marilyn soon began reaching beyond her own age and experience in a number of poems for radio. She meticulously researched *Grandfather was a Soldier* by walking every foot of soil the Canadian Third Battalion fought over in World War I. Those few who remember that war know that she was uncannily accurate.

In *Laika and Folchakov* her reach was even longer—beyond time and space. As I listened to it on the CBC, I thought, 'she knows no boundaries, no failure of the imagination will ever stop her, there is nothing we cannot expect from her'. The two hemispheres of her brain appear to be equally developed—her hardheaded logicality is balanced by a sideways-seeing that seems close to clairvoyance.

In her recent work I see a latter-day Blake—
not his *Songs of Innocence and Experience* but his enormous,
baffling, beautiful, prophetic books. *The Mind's Road to Love*
reads like a modern Genesis, biblical in its language, erotic as
The Song of Solomon. Yet, for all these equivalencies, Bowering's
voice is contemporary. It might even be 'the future poetry'
foreseen by Sri Aurobindo.

P.K. Page

The Mind's Road to Love

1.
In the evening I found you,
a man on a stoop reading

while the life of the forest rose
around him.

In the morning I found you again,
sleeping, while the sun scoured

the hills to brightness,
until at noon I climbed into my spirit.

I saw you through a mirror,
and the mirror was three thousand miles,

and the mirror was a telephone,

but I was blinded by the mirror
and by its shadows,

and I did not see the light of noon
on your face,

I did not find your body in the forest,
or in the sea,

or with my body.

I read all the books,
and I sat on the stoop where I had found you

reading, and I thought of how the books made steps
up a mountain,

Marilyn Bowering

and I saw truth in the mirror of words,
and in a face that changed hourly

to a beast, a woman, a man, a child,
to a charitable angel,

to the face of God (He or She) turning away from me.
A ladder fell down from a cloud

as from a spaceship: I began to climb the ladder
rung by rung.

I gave up food and drink,
I took off my wedding ring,

I began to think of the actual
existence of things:

and I saw the species range themselves in order,
with the birds at the top of the ladder,

and at the foot the microbes,
and I saw the human family ascending

and descending as if they were angels,
and the angels were pushed aside,

and I saw that the ladder was a tree in a garden,
and that it required care and feeding and pruning,

and I saw you asleep at the foot of the tree;
and then I saw you speak into the telephone,

and the spaceship descend and the birds feed you.

You looked up. Then the whole world was made
out of nothing,

but the books described its beauty,
and the mathematics measured it,

and with the measuring came power
and lightning, and I flew

to the top of the tree as a bird.
I entered into every species—

human kind ascending and descending,
the great mammals and all the extinct creatures—

the mammoths and the unicorns—
and I made living creatures from stars and stones

and aluminum; I strung telephone wires
and formed networks of fibreoptics,

and lightning made the whole of creation spin,
until it was magnetic,

and the earth attracted the moon and the planets
and I saw the splendour of that whirling,

the turning sea, the spin of blood and fluid
through my body,

the great circle of the trees of the forest,
your arms as they wrapped around me.

But he or she who does not praise is
struck dumb,

so I opened my lips and applied my heart
to my vision of you as it came.

Marilyn Bowering

About Your Name

5.
If you wish to think about what is invisible,
you start with a loved one,

with their essence, with the touch of lips
in actuality or in potential: as beginning with

electrons and moving to electricity,
and the hydro electric dams on the rivers,

and the changes of names they undergo
according to politics—that is, you ignore history.

As to the way things are—this is intelligible
only through a vision of you.

Marvellous colours that are invisible except
to the naked eye, unseen by electronic pulses,

or by mirrors, or by angels talking and drawing
each other's pictures,

unseen by all except me, who happened to find you
in the right place and time.

Because when I look at you I seem to see nothing:
I see the sweetness and light that is above

and beyond all mirrors or the hair combing of angels,
or the polishings of motor cars and mountain bicycles:

it is greatest because it is the simplest, and because it is full
like the air, of the intention to touch.

For that which is most actual is you when I see you
and when I am with you.

You ask how this came about:
it is a question of grace, not practice,

a step in the right direction by chance,
a desire, not thought.

And I meditated on the mind's ascent to love
the whole world before me, and all the roads,

and I waited for you.

In the summer of 1996 I was invited to give a writing workshop in the Muskoka region north of Toronto. The first night the organizer gave me a list of people who had enrolled in my workshop, including JIM CLARKE, a Supreme Court Justice of Ontario. Up until that point, the only writing I'd read by a judge was a document as thick as the Toronto telephone directory headed "Reasons on Sentencing". It was creative, as my convicted husband could attest, but a long way from being poetry.

It is every writer's dream: you give a workshop, someone hands you a manuscript, you read it right away (it's what you're being paid to do) but suddenly, it's no effort anymore. You are reading for pleasure. You can't put it down. It's raw. Driven. There's a fresh voice. A perspective you've never considered. You laugh. Weep. It's so good you know you can show it to your publisher. Within a year this writer will publish his first book.

What struck me, when I initially read Jim Clarke's poems, was his enormous capacity for compassion. He writes with wry humour too, on just about every subject from bicycle theft to love. The poems in this book let us peek under Madame Justice's blindfold, giving us a rare glimpse of her concerned, but very human face.

Life has not always been "just" to James Clarke, himself. He began writing poetry ten years ago, when his wife of twenty-five years took her own life at Niagara Falls, leaving him with six children and a lifetime of questions she would never be able to answer.

James Clarke continues to produce; he studies his craft and he keeps getting better. This fall he published his fourth volume, *The Way Everyone Is Inside*. Sylvia Plath's, "The blood-jet is poetry/ there is no stopping it," could have been written about Jim.

Susan Musgrave

Silver Mercies

"It takes seven years for a suicide,"
the priest said, but I was too numb

to hear his words: that was the black
spring tongues of tulips pierced my

heart and the thought of never seeing
her again was more than I could bear.

Last night when her long beautiful
arms reached across the bed, huge with

desire, and I could not even remember her
voice, that rich resonance that once filled

our home with warmth and joy, I grieved for
all our faithless flesh too small for

even strongest love; but snow,
our comforter, knows us better than

ourselves and covers us whitely, seven
times seven, with soft forgetfulness, and

just as the hibiscus never completely fades
but rises red and radiant always

in our mind, so too the snowy voices
of those we loved live on in our reborning

selves, silver mercies of the dead.

James Clarke

The End of Something

Why did the waiting always seem so long?
All day she had tiptoed around
the apartment as though he was already

there, sleeping somewhere, and the
least noise would waken him. She made
herself tea for the fourth time,
sat on the edge of the beige couch in the
living room, knees clapped together. She could

hear the faucet dripping in the kitchen,
a fly buzzing at the window pane. She
went over, drew back the curtain.
He parked the blue Pontiac in
front of the apartment and let it idle

a few minutes before he got out. She
always spotted his leather cowboy boots
first, slipping out of the door,
two black daggers. She remembered
the first time he had ordered her to take

off her sweater and bra. "Nice tits," he said
staring at her small, white body.
All she could recall
was his shallow, rapid breathing,
the rancid smell of his oily skin

and the bluntless of his knee
wedging apart her legs. When he was
finished he strolled around the apartment as
though nothing had happened. "It's a pigsty
in here Jeannie," he said.

She could never look him
in the eye and her only
recollection of their brief encounters was
the skull and crossbones on his silver
buckle, the black cowboy boots, and
riff of his zipper. She felt like
carrion, the same deadweight feeling she had
back home in Nova Scotia when he used to
sneak upstairs to her bedroom

after Mum and Dad were asleep and she would
stare at the dark ceiling, heart pounding,
waiting for his rough hands to reach
under the cover to touch her body.

Today she knelt on the Chinese rug
on the living room floor, arms
criss-crossed over her chest,
waiting for the knock.

That evening when her boyfriend found her
she was still there,
speared by slanting light,
moaning like a golden doe.

How to Bribe a Judge

Snap to attention when he enters the
courtroom and never fail to say:
"GOOD MORNING."

Smile—make him feel welcome as a lover.

Laugh heartily at all his jokes even when
they're incomprehensible.

When he says something particularly absurd
chime in: "I wish I'd thought of that."

Ponder deeply—learn the art of furrowing the
brow or staring gravely at the ceiling—
especially when he's talking silly.

Without appearing obsequious finish every
sentence with "My Lord."

Quote with boldness from his old decisions
no matter how dull, irrelevant or wrong.

When he's patently confused interject:
"Would you mind repeating that My Lord,
I missed the subtlety of it." Or try a
variation: "You're one step ahead of me
as usual My Lord."

Tell him his judgments are novel, break
new ground. Avoid meretricious adjectives
like "brilliant"; he'll know it's flattery.

Send him a Christmas card, expressing
gratitude for his birth.

Never offer cash—his dignity will be
slighted.

Finally, never appeal his judgments.

A Young Offender

He was only 18,
with the babyface of a teenager
when he appeared before me
charged with 12 counts
of armed robbery.

During the bail hearing he stared through me
as though
I were glass.

Not once did his eyes
betray the blue fury
inside him even when
I refused bail.

Yes, he would go away for a while
but I knew he'd be back,
older and deadlier,
and I was scared,
the same dread the crew
of the Enola Gay felt
as they dropped their dark and
awkward child on a dreaming city.

James Clarke

You know when you read CARLA FUNK's poems that she's smart and muse-ridden; you may not know that she's also a mother, a superior baker, a seamstress and a teacher—and she's only in her twenties. Her competence can be quite frightening to those of us who can barely sew on a button or bake a loaf of bread that should be eaten instead of sold at Beaver Lumber for building material. From the time I first met her when she was a student in a second-year workshop at the University of Victoria, I knew I'd run into a major talent.

Her poems are remarkable in their ability to slide between the secular and sacred with so much ease that you hardly know they've taken you on such a splendid voyage. Carla moves seamlessly from her own father into the arms of God. Possessed with the pragmatism, spirituality and sensuousness of a St. Theresa of Avila, in one poem she can pair "the architecture of desire" and the "omniscient darkness" with flatulence and the picking of scabs. Even in her earliest work, she came to words with a sense of their oral richness; she knows how to make them sing on the page. If every poem, as Robert Bly says, is a journey of the soul, her poems take us on long journeys to places we couldn't have predicted. There's music all around us and things that were once familiar are wonderfully changed: they're more intense and luminous than they were before. That's one of the many reasons to treasure Carla Funk.

Lorna Crozier

Disclaimer

When I say "my father" I might mean
the man who came to the hospital two hours late
peered into the nursery window
and declared me the ugliest baby he'd ever seen.
Or I might mean the God into whose arms
I want to crawl on those broken
empty room nights.

And when I say "mother"
and the mother says "daughter"
and the daughter sounds a lot like me,
any resemblance is purely chance,
poetic coincidence.

When the mother in the poem says things like
"if you play with your belly button
you'll come untied, zoom wildly
around the room like a deflating balloon,
end up a loose sack of flesh on the floor,"
neither the poem nor the daughter
quite believes her.

When I say "daughter"
I might mean the one I dreamed to be,
long-legged, narrow-hipped with lips
that pout and smile simultaneously.

When I call you beautiful
I might be harbouring resentment.

When my hands at the night's bright screen
type out "your hands" there is a certain amount
of longing, sometimes a thousand
handfuls, sometimes more.

Carla Funk

When I write "evening" I'm usually thinking
a teenager's version of the night, the omniscient
darkness and two kids
all eager mouth and hands
on the living room floor
until six in the morning
when the girl realizes
she's made a huge mistake,
this isn't the kind of guy she'd marry
and it's too late, time doesn't rewind
like the stupid action movie they rented
and never got around to watching.
(If only, if only she'd insisted on a romance.)

When the poem aims for romance
it leaves behind hickeys and groping,
favours the architecture of desire,
a house of skin and bone.

When I write "husband" I sometimes mean
the kind I have
and other times the kind I won't:
the ones who claim never
to have picked a scab and enjoyed it
and the ones who punctuate
their own jokes with flatulence.

(When I say "flatulence" I mean what I say.)

When I write about the physical body,
I try not to get too attached.

For example, when I say "breast"
I mean it in its most useful form
and when I write of nakedness I want to hide
behind someone fully clothed.

When I write "you" I mean you in the black shirt
with the comfortable shoes, you who feels all eyes
in the room riveted on your every breath and move.
What will you say when you open your mouth?
When the words become lies and the lies
wear the names of people I know
I want to believe they are secretly proud,
leave the room and page thinking
that poem is about me, she means me,
I want her to mean me.

Psalm of thirst

The sun like a burning eye stares
until the river shrivels into lines
and all that remains of the rainy season
is a watering hole sludged with elephant dung
the air a banner of gnats and tsetse flies

as the deer longs for water
so much more the creatures of this place
who bear the blueprint of thirst
in their bone-dry bellies

in this open throat of dry land
the island blends into the plain
and grown pelicans nesting there
begin to leave in search of water
while the young flightless ones left behind
walk over the cracked clay for days
until their charcoal bodies give out
fleck the baked landscape
in small feathered heaps

*

I'm thirsty the man says
in the early morning heat on the hill
the first rays of sun swelling the horizon

in his mouth the weight of a whole earth
a thick coat of dust lining his throat

to his lips the hyssop branch
soaked with gall   that final drink
swallowing all the light from this place

*

32   Introductions ...poets present poets

As deep calls to deep
in the immeasurable electricity of God
so thirst calls to water
the dry-tongued stones licking
the morning air   desperate
a man stumbling across
the sun-scorched sand
the word *oasis* a cold pool
of hope in his mouth

so the porous heart soaks up
what rain and goodness he sends

so my deserts turn to gardens
in the presence of the Lord

Messengers

All mouth and throbbing with the need to
speak they arrive, heels printing into the earth
a colon: the introduction of much
to come. They stand outside
dreams at the foot of your bed, scrolls of their tongues
unfurling, important, blessed tongues
written with indelible ink.

(What does it feel like to carry God's
tongue in your mouth? A single word light
as a dandelion spore, heavy as gold
brick?) Lantern throats glow each breath.

*Listen. Someone is dying. Even this
made beautiful.*
                        *Proclaim the glory of everyday
life, bruises and the sweet flesh of earlobe. Swallow
the love you are given.*
                        *Hear me. Unto you a gift is given, no
strings attached. You are favoured. You are
whole.*
                *Fall on your face and seek wine in the dry
valley. Find flesh among bones. Miracles
are prepared for the tasting.*

And you startle at their voices, each
syllable a fire-fly in the ear, flicker and spark
upon waking. This may have been a dream, this
may have been more.

T o write is, in some gauge, to be *misled*. To let language and our history of language (literatures, *contes*, tales) mislead us. As SUSAN HOLBROOK does, letting even pronunciation mislead her: she always read the word "misled" as "myzled," past tense of the verb "to misle!"

To chart a wayward course in words—this, to me, is the best of what poetry can bring us, its double-sided coin of delight and wound, cherish and forbid.

Holbrook's first book charts a course through forms that won't settle quietly into their "genres": prose moves in and through poetry and becomes... poetry! Holbrook delights in language's spill: its willingness and freedom to exceed the logic of "the said" or the "conveyable" that simply aims to reach the "understood." She doesn't ask that false question "what does it mean?" but rather "what does it provoke?", or "what does it site and cite?"

"Sense" in poetry is not just "information." It's tonality, play, the slippage always in language that makes it resist fixed meanings and repel fixed "cathartic" effects (which are finally just manipulative of the reader, not *inviting* him or her). Holbrook aims for delight and never for instruction. And she's done her reading too: her work shimmers and refracts other, earlier readings and texts. The excerpt here takes on this task playfully (yet sombrely), seguing from lines of Grimm's Fairy Tales (where curious forthright girls do not, I daresay, meet good ends) into the present day's kazooming katacylsmic kaleidoscope of images, rhythms, words, scopic splendours... How do we live? How do we ever *stay alive*?

And what I like is that Holbrook doesn't give us the answers. She just deepens the questions so that they resonate more fully, grabbing me, insisting and snickering at the same time, letting me decide. Me, reader.

Erin Mouré

from **Grim**

*Then she was forced to put on the red-hot shoes, and dance until she dropped down dead.**

Fortissimo romance, blistered to the max. Rather be ghoulish than girlish, or take salts and calm the fever, sitz baths drown out the whinnying. The subject of pathos or bathos or Cheerios. The Spanish soap opera interrupted by an ad for *peenay sol* and a tree burst through the roof. Stole the show. Narrative is all fun and games until someone loses a roof. Come-uppance is no coin, a warning no prism. And does taking too long to smooth the chenille fall between the cracks of lust and sloth. It's not in grace but in a burning house that we say there is a god. The creepy guy sold me cinnamon gum, saying *so you like* Big Red.

*Italicized lines are gratefully stolen from *The Complete Grimm's Fairy Tales* (New York: Pantheon Books, 1944).

One of them noticed a gold ring on the little finger of the murdered girl and, as it would not come off at once, he took an axe and cut her finger off. But it sprang into the air, over the cask, and fell straight into the bride's bosom.

Paying for packaging. The meanings of cleaving, the digital sound of collateral booty. Is this a lesbian episode. Violence the big tip-off. The admission of certain "feelings" stalling the ceremony. If bosom is singular, how could it fall in, how conceal a scissors. You may now give her the finger. Dotted trajectories score freeze-framed villains, floor X'd with duct tape. Released due to the improbability of the facts. Disbelief, clemency, bugs in a rug. More than duende, jock itch and jiggers spur haunting. This doesn't feel like popcorn. Her finger the memento mori of functional value. How often is duct tape used for ducts.

Then said he: "*Wife, now that you are Pope, be satisfied, you cannot become anything greater.*" "*I will consider about that,*" *said she.*

The offhand comment that chipmunks don't make good leaders. And a couple right there in the yard. Nerve, cheek, balls, gall. Carving. Under that hat you'll find a nut. In that nut ambition rattles. In the rattle a flake of pepper traversed by a mite dreaming of becoming the pope. An indefinite article precedes the rest of us. Best of all, consider about ring kisses. King-sized seats. Quotes open and close around your every poop. Said the satisfied, said the become. Crave bothered touch. Hot doves loitering about her toilette. Implored he, "Forget thunder, douche." Flap and lathered.

Susan Holbrook

> "Yes," answered the cat, "you will enjoy it as much as you would enjoy sticking that dainty tongue of yours out the window."

It's the house with pink wimpling. Wet bell. A big French kiss for summer, blow November. Out the gopher hole of experience comes the furtive muster. Packing lustre, lick trust. Assuming all her life that sticking her tongue out was an invitation, by now her dainty heart hung about her heels. Dragging scowls. Knowing another's enjoy. Another joy, another jolly. Shutters akimbo. Creaking thighs anticipate dollar days, an address to the street, the casement itself answering yes.

After a while, a second giant took the drummer, and stuck him in his button-hole.

Tender little drummer. High-hat meringue. The sparing a close call: had the giant preferred hooks. Had the giant already a boutonnière. What would gender do. Bouffant, slouch, the east side of the shirt. Pacemaker. Want darling?—the drummer's own buttonholes. Kitten paper. A giant's head always North. Does bigness or smallness make a hand paw-like. In other words, for whom will you cry if the rescue fails.

I first encountered the caustic yet dreamy voice of SUZETTE MAYR when, on a hot autumnal day in Halifax, NS, in 1995, I wandered into exquisitely leftist Red Herring Books and began to scan *Moon Honey*, her just-published debut novel about a 'white' girl who turns 'brown.' Being a honey-coloured Haligonian, exultantly 'African' and Mi'kmaq (with some vanilla in the mocha), I knew about the twists of racial identity, and I was curious to see how a black-brown Calgarian woman treats these experiences. Reading *Moon Honey*, a fascinating union of Ovid's *Metamorphoses* and that Bible of US Liberalism, John Howard Griffin's *Black Like Me* (1961), I conjured apt, answering adverbs: deftly, imaginatively, poetically, politically. When assembling my anthology, *Eyeing the North Star: Directions in African-Canadian Literature* (1997), I read Mayr's poetry chapbook, *Zebra Talk* (1991), which, semi (but tantalizingly)-autobiographically, explores the emotions of being raised German (white) and Caribbean (black) in urban Alberta, a complex deal demanding no-bullshit, pomo grooves. So, in all Mayr's stuff, prose and poetry, there's a ferociously forensic trial of race and racism, sex and sexism, and *femme*-eroticism and homophobia. (She say all that mess ya don't like, chief!) Mayr backs her theses with startling conjunctions of biological and material (consumer decor) metaphors. It's like watching Jean-Michel Basquiat cannibalize *Martha Stewart*.

Born in 1967, Mayr anchored my anthology as its youngest contributor. Along with poet Wayde Compton and poet-novelist David Odhiambo, she fronts a fresh generation of West Coast African-Canadian *avant-gardistes*. A *protegeé* of Alberta writer Aritha van Herk, Mayr has imbibed her mentor's sardonic feminism, but, like Compton, she scrutinizes a biracial identity, and, like Odhiambo, she inks a finely bebop-textured poetry, injecting surreal moments into hyper-real contexts, and matching highly visual images with syncopated form. Her closest Afro-USian model is Harryette Mullen (see S*PeRM**K*T [1992]); her closest Canadian model is....? Mayr's ideology be kinda like progressive Josephine Bakeresque (see Mayr's "To Her rainbow tribe").

Mayr's tone be part tonic water and part disinfectant. Fore you relax under imagery of coconut trees, she show you a big ol half-squashed cockroach. You want a Benetton ad, rainbow fuckfest, she give you pix of the Holocaust or photos of "Blood stains slave-hewn steps..." She use a tough vernacular, witchy, butchy, exact and exacting. She like to pun (so 'Canajun', that): "A grandfather flower-potted in a German grave yard"; butter served with "yeast infections" or "Vitamin E. Coli"; "Mayderdees" blending *maître de* with Chef Boyardee. Mayr refer slyly to Pop too: Her lines, "How to ice the cake of regret/ someone left out in the rain," diss that silly, LSD-era anthem, "MacArthur Park."

There you have it: Mayr is the upsetting upstart in Anglo-Canuck poetry, if you got ears to hear. She is black—*and beautiful*—and bursting (blossoming?) with truth. She recognizes *angst* in the domestic and the diurnal: the antifreeze slipped into yer decaf, the broken razor blades slid into yer Timbits. You got to handle her poetry with care! Her lines are barbed-wire, sugar-frosted.

George Elliott Clarke

Across oceans

A grandfather flower-potted in a German grave yard around his plot is blotting paper for steel wool tears. Next door is the war monument. Another the other his brother grandfather ours this time is unpotted and scattered by shell and shrapnel. He is grass this monument is made of grass our grandmother nightly makes love to grass.

Another the other grandmother also made of grass but also sand and the sun that slaps the faces of blind white tourists. Blood stains slave-hewn steps the kiss of palm tree ocean. Tropical ferns grow from concrete and empty vodka bottles. Stone chews through our family's blood.

Two mixed.
Too violent.

Visiting my mother's country:
An albino pit bull lives next door

Patter of palm tree leaves sounds rain on concrete
sees her first giant cockroach
its abdomen cracked under her uncle's shoe its head crushed
under her mother's book its sweeping antennae still wave
hello
spit-warm water from the tap tastes of salt of sweat
walls crawl geckoes and banana trees snakes
her body drips and smells of ocean
pigments sprout sweat-flowers
her hair frizzes undone

During breakfast she eyes White Girl, the albino pit bull next door, over a bowl of Cheerios. White Girl resents the barbed wire fence that separates them but eats yesterday's leftover snapper and grits without complaining. Last week she ate the head off a newborn puppy and let out a long, squeaky belch. Welcome, she says, aware a stranger's come to town. Welcome.

Married girlfriends (i)

That crusted animal in the freezer next to all the other shames
tin foiled beef bourguignon to go along with nylon brassieres
back when the butter still smelled of vacation
instead of yeast infections.

How predictable can someone be before
she's   freezer burn?

Marinate the ache. Angelfood scoots over the counter chased
by the frosting gun. How to ice the cake of regret someone left
out in the rain? Not cake at all but styrofoam insemination.

                                             This
fatigue of MSG and the nipples dolloped on her lovely chest
  arch between husbands, wives and the wives' girlfriends.
  Tupperware compartments the fine edge between lunch and
  garbage. Drink wine not for the romance but for the iron in
  the grape skins. Transmute into the chugging tunnels of shit
  (the rage of endives)
                                            Vitamin E. Coli

Love letters and butts float in decaf
Is she with   anyone at all?
Your ass too   icy.
Excavate   here.

Married girlfriends (ii)

Valentine's Day a rush of
origami aorta auricles lips of sphincters
and murmur-clicks of escaped blood prisons

The restaurant closes when he says so. There
have been happier Mayderdees.
Complicit germs on dollar bills, ridged edges of
coins lace the table. A wife's girlfriend is not
as glorious as camembert or organ meat seasoned
in cracked pepper, garlic, vinegar, and salt. Wife scrapes her
    frizzled onions to the side. Butter
wouldn't melt in *her* gun.

Valentine's Day uxorious sad sex only only a holiday
for martyrs. She resurrects her sadness. Inevitable
tally of the evening: 1000 cranes folded and creased.

To Her *rainbow tribe*

The lieutenant in the banana skirt dances the dance of the
rainbow to the harmonized grunts of meat-beating racists.
They watch and they lick; the ripple of orchestral strings
the tendons the muscles the bananas and the snorts of
    bravo.
Bravo. Fattened fingers strangled by female holes of gold
strike palms in time to her radiating hips and stage lights
miss the arches of light in the drops of bodywater flicked
from her scalp to her souls.

bag woman plants her oldened butt on the steps of her
    castle.
nested in milk-cartons and ghosts of coconut half-shells.
    Queen
evicted from her fortress turn turn turn Josephine show us
your withered chocolate butt still worth bravo and swing
    swing
swing them goddamn bananas. Fingers gaggled with bands
of gold make her a tight necklace of flesh and dollar bills
    throw sequins onto bloodshot eyes. For the last time
    watch the R. Negre
queen dance. For the first time know that she owns rainbows
    and
for all time know that she/fucks/you don't matter no more

Rob mclennan was born in Ottawa on March 15, 1970, adopted and in January of the next year moved to a farm near Maxville, Ontario. He returned to Ottawa in 1989.

He watched "far too much television" when he was young and wanted to own a restaurant when he was ten. He owns over 5,000 comic books and has, he says, "no patience for halfway."

mclennan is the author of five books of poems and thirty-seven poetry chapbooks. He has edited "a handful of anthologies" and runs above/ground press.

In 1999 he was short-listed for the Archibald Lampman Award and the Shaunt Basmajian Award and he has won the Canadian Authors' Association/Air Canada Award as the most promising writer in Canada under thirty.

Statement: "I dont think I write because I 'have things to say'. No one has that many things to say; to me the questions are always more important than the answers and construction is as arbitrary & important as the next thing."

John Newlove

barely moving, barely thinking

they advertise in the place of day, cool quarters
held against the heat of flesh

students all the same brown hat, but not
a card among them, the scene you know
when visa thru

i hold my heart up for a drink: it goes

journal entry: i dont need you / i just want you

rob mclennan

milk

the carcass of the old house after she moved
to the apartment. damp,
& rot. was the only one i knew who made
tomato soup w/

milk, the cloudy white stirrd in

slowly, continuous. uncle bob crushing premium plus
w/ his spoon. renovated the kitchen & the back after

husband died, his winter body brought in
after discovery in the snow, lay there cold
& stiff on the table

until the ambulance arrived, knowing
they neednt hurry. this much

is sure, is what

i know, how long

years can reach out thru, from
behind, & grab

at your neck like you were seven a second time,
scanning magazines in the wrong part

of another uncles house, black marks

over the parts of the female anatomy you knew,
even then, were interesting.

stones & ice: a translation

i am unable to translate skin. some languages
lose / adverse to shifts
in other states.

like stones, not ice. i touch, & touches me.
a prophecy built for state of mind.

her skin is like. her breasts are like.
when telling, & no longer showing.

stones: my father has fields full. every time
a blade thru the soil, hits.

ice: melts on her skin. doesnt change
the taste but the texture. goosebumps.

the restoration of st peters

the newest trend in rome, they write,
to improve historical buildings. make them
look nice.

120,000 cubic metres of scaffolding
are hard to contradict.

newly painted, of scrubbd marble
, of ochre, green & red.

you make an arguement for peace of mind.
you make an arguement for something.

for continuity. an exterior decorators catalog
, what once was uniform, if dirty, colour.

errol flynns last lover

breaking 40 years of silence & bad stigma,
well after his swash & buckle days.

dying of everything in vancouver, a failure
made complete—of liver, heart.

like malcolm lowry, death by misadventure,
an accidental yankee caught for good.

theres love at seventeen & then theres this, the starlet
& the alcoholic cad, old misfit.

the magic of life & bigger than, shrunk down to copy,
when none of it matters. never did.

as the couple lands in canada, 1959, the final stop
in all adventuring. the airplane touching earth.

Amazing, friends. Not one of the initial fifty-two poems in GEORGE MURRAY's brilliantly stacked deck of playing-cards, *Carousel: A Book of Second Thoughts*, begins with, 'I.' Only the final, fifty-third poem, 'The Joker's Last Words' does so: and just might speak with the mordant authorial voice. Which says, 'I always wanted to read a eulogy for first thoughts, / the ones that got away, truth being rootless as / the shadow of a bird in flight;' thus returning the trumped reader to the book's wild card beginning with a fanned flourish of assurance that there is life, and to boot, after death—if it is another's.

What a benison when, as Richard Wilbur recently remarked, 'The standard awful poetry of the last forty years has been a sort of artless diary entry in free verse.' Instead Murray directs his considerable abilities—nerves of mercury; a hares-breath-acute ear for inner and outer voices in all discovered weathers; an enhanced power of (seemingly inexhaustible) exuberant invention; a funambulist's uncanny balance on rhythms collecting and flexing their larval strengths; a prestidigitator's sleight-of-time; a swift, protean intelligence coupled with a sickled-wicked wit;—to his first true love, the play of language! Well, no lesser talent could pull off a poem titled 'The Cardiologist's Arrest', with scene-of-the-crime notes by 'a poetic policeman.' Or would risk 'The Eschatologist's End'; let alone begin 'The Numerologist's Obituary' with, 'Sullying quantum physics at Harvard...' *Sullying* quantum physics! Oh there is balm in Gilead, friends, and George Murray is its canny chapman. Step right up!

It is not often that a reader may feel of a collection of verse, that one's favourite is surely the poem that one is reading. *Carousel* is a book to own, treasure, read to tatters and seldom lend. And there is much more to come. Let me tempt you with this from a large selection of uncollected work, a poem of a bird and a bird of a poem wherein Murray writes, 'It's the legs / that betrayed you— / thin as thread and / knotted into tiny rosettes, / virtually weightless.'

Richard Outram

The Lion Tamer's Embalming

Some called him *totemic* (a tamer with a bit of the lion
in him), others a saprophyte; yet regardless, you can all
guess how he went & it wasn't pretty, neither the act
nor the conundrum of burial: his half-corpse forcing us
to kill the beast, spill its belly in the Three Ring dirt
to retrieve the missing pieces needed to finish the puzzle
(sad, he had been so proud of being a simple man in life);
but what came pouring out looked largely uniform,
the bloody pre-performance feed suddenly so similar to
the man himself (a mess of blue digestive juices), so we
voted to defer the decision & bury them together, send
them on as a *symbiot*: the lion & his tamer, each with a bit
of the other inside, trust that whoever received them
was more suited than we to judge what belonged to whom.

George Murray

The Palmist's Elegy

Right until her death at ninety-three she stood steadfast by
a belief that the skin was simply a record, that with a little
effort fate could be realigned however one desired: *You
have a great future behind you, she often joked, lines on
the palm shift over time like tide rills on a beach*; yet even
she passed, old & crippled, survived only by a skeptical
spouse & six dubious children who bore silently
the eccentricities of her life: the incense, crystals, scented
candles, the quiet, level flutes; & while somewhere in
the eulogy it was suggested that where she was she could
finally be young again, her aged beau, so covered in wrinkles
that he read like a map, looked doubtful, was even seen
to examine his hand as the casket closed, no doubt
    wondering
whether, if it weren't for time, she would recognize him now.

The Mountebank's Wake

The party only really got going once the mourners
(conveniently given to bouts of hypochondria &
loud displays) cut into the sack of specifics, tonics
& restoratives, emptying the chunky brown bottles
into a large crucible where, on closer inspection,
it was discovered that every potion was essentially
booze: vodka with mugwort for the knocky knees,
gin spiked with harebell for croup, wild turkey
with a pinch of garlic for dum-dum fever, rubbing
alcohol laced with the slightest taste of arsenic
for hiccups; yet while some scoffed (claiming
his dubious, sometimes lethal, physics were only
cures for *funereal disease*), up until the new dawn
broke, everyone else seemed to be feeling just fine.

The Somnambulist's Burial

At the funeral everyone kept expecting him
to rise, to jump out of the coffin
& traipse about the room, use his glassy,
dead eyes to wink at the frightened
minister & read passages from the Bible
he could now personally discredit;

but instead they just buried him,
upright as was his wont, left a bell
to ring in case of a false alarm, in case
this great traveler of sleep found
something different down there
in the darkness of soil, something
that might turn him up out of his rest &
set him to walking urgently from the bed.

The Coroner's Autopsy

Found in a pool of blood below the examination table,
murder was ruled out when his colleagues opened
him like a doctor's bag,
                         a loud snap with a sterile jack
to the solar plexus, gloved hands reaching into
the black cavity, the ribs raising on either side
like a crackling drawbridge, pulled up to reveal
the surprising cause of death: exsanguination,
an evacuation of blood from the body as though
the heart gave one great pump, sent every drop of him
out the mouth, ears, nose, eyes, anus, urethra;
no foul play, just the natural holes with which
he was born rebelling in a sudden, overwhelming
case of the willies, a much needed release after
years of casual judgement in the presence of death.

ELIZABETH PHILIPS' language is a balm to the ear. No one is more aware of the music in words, of their roll, glide and rumble. She is a nature poet in the best sense of the word. She walks into the open landscape that is her home and sees what many of us miss, from the smallest blade of grass to the bed of a deer. Like Mary Oliver, her journeys into the natural world take her close to the invisible and spiritual, which she respectfully circles and names. She is equally attentive to the human. Her elegies tug at the heart, but she balances grief with passion and love. Her poems luxuriate in the sexual. Like the orange in the poem included here, her words tempt you to bite in and savour. Their taste satisfies a longing you didn't even know you had.

Patrick Lane

Orange

I want the orange
you are eating. I know
I could have had my own, you offered

one from the bowl, but I want
yours, and laughing, you feed
it to me, section by section, until

my mouth is full, the pursed
sweetness opens
and I swallow it. The orange

is as fine as I thought
it might be, acid bound to sugar in a skin of
barely skin, the pleasure not just

in the fruit, but in the taste of your finger-
tips, the bitterness
of where you've been. Where

have you been? In the garden
gathering marigolds, Persian
zinnias, that's where I

would have you, but the goodness
is also in what is not quite
delectable, dry summer heat, the peel

shuttered in your palm, my bare
shoulders, and all
I cannot consume, sorrel

distances, your eyes
on mine, and then the shift,
the looking away.

Elizabeth Philips

Meditation On Chuang-tzu
(for Patrick)

The goldfish I have called
Chuang-tzu, after the Chinese sage,
chases along the surface of the water
sifting for scraps of food.
Isolated from the school by sickness,
by grey threads of fungus
that grow on his fins like mould
on bread, he is confined to five gallons,
a clump of java moss, gravel
and one smooth black stone.

Even in sickness he is full-
hearted, swims a spiral dance
carving out of water
his own kingdom, a world without
edges. He sucks greedily there
balanced on the sweeping
butterfly of his tail, catching
small mouthfuls of bright air.
The medicine has failed to cure him
and yet he grows, a stout
gleaming oranda, each scale
a finely etched oval of bronze light.

From my desk where I read
Chuang-tzu, I look up as the oranda
plunges to the bottom, shimmying hard
then resting, only to float up again
effortlessly, like a balloon
let go.

Chuang-tzu says, "if water is clear
when it is tranquil, how much more so
the spirit?" And I imagine him,
an old man straying into a strange wood,
distracted, on a new path.
Surprised by the pool at his feet
he stops and peers down at his own face
reflected. His eyes
are two perfect moons, and he sees in them
the stillness he has been seeking
all his life, an emptiness
to which all things must gravitate.

But then the goldfish, the life of the pond,
rise to meet his shadow, shattering
his moment of vision, sight
distorted once more
by the roiling spirit of the water,
tame fish wild in hunger and the light
on the water broken, refracted
by the swift congregation of fish
stirring as one body, one
open mouth.

Elizabeth Philips

On the Path of the Deer

I am following the path of the deer through spruce
and down into pine, glimpsing now and again the blue
flash of a jay flapping from tree to tree.

I am going deeper into the wood on a trace hammered sound
by the passing of hooves, to the place
where seven beds are pressed out of the snow, seven hollows

glazed by the warm bellies of sleeping deer. I take the path
away from the quiet hall where last summer my friend
called after me and laughed

and caught me up. But he never followed me here,
never saw the marks where soft mouths of deer grazed
the tender bark of young trees.

His long stride never left me breathless
beneath this sprawling pine. I am tracking the way of the deer
beyond the range of his beckoning on the day that I turned

and met his green gaze. And yet
I hear him ahead of me now, his feet singing on the trail
in the twilight of the trees, and though I go with great care

I cannot catch him up. His laugh hovers in the air
above the last bend, and surely I will not be lost
or without blessing if he allows me

to see him just this once leaping after the deer on the path
that leads to sleeping in circles of snow in the heart
of the wood.

Every strong poetry has its own distinctive flavour or tang, the combination of qualities that makes it unique. To introduce KAREN SOLIE's poetry to a new reader, a person is naturally inclined to say 'here, try some of this,' and hand her the equivalent of a small glass of single malt. Then we could stand around and try words like smoky or peaty or big nose with a complex middle and a touch of diesel in the endgame. But an intro is an intro so I'll venture something like this: before I encountered Karen Solie's work the idea of encountering both Sylvia Fricker and Susan Sontag in the same sensibility was an idle notion. But here it is—a fierce writing of quickness and edge that can take on just about anything: the highway, Freud, farm suicides, sturgeon, all manner of flawed and far-off romance—with candour and a trenchant humour that's the cutting edge of intelligence. Not to mention sly skinny music, not to mention sheer metaphorical pounce, moves that accomplish themselves before you realize they're underway. No telegraphing (as my basketball coach used to shout at us, vainly, from the sidelines), no redundancy, no fumbling from line to line. Do we recognize this coffee shop?

> Inside, frying is a kind of weather, a Florida
> for flies, the doughnuts afflicted,
> the coffee malicious.
> Tiny friendless salads make you weep.

Lord, yes. As we recognize—even when we haven't seen them first hand—that boyfriend's car ("Black Nova. Jacked up.

Fast."), that Day's Inn, those bleak gas stations and solitary rooms, all of them viewed with an intensity that burns away nostalgia and sentiment. Maybe, tossing around words in that kitchen of the mind, we'd come up with something like "W.O. Mitchell's shadow self" or a recall of Jack Gilbert's observation that God is compassionate but not merciful. Karen Solie's work reminds me that there is at the heart of metaphor a delicious amoral joy, that raw irrepressible humour often personified in the trickster which kicks in no matter how 'painful' or 'depressing' the subject. Lord, yes, we say, the hangover.

> Now, the day is explicit.
> Swallows fall in shrieks
> from great heights. My head
> is a drawer full of spoons.

I asked my friend Barry Dempster what he thought was the special quality of Karen's work and he said maybe it's a combination of a remarkably dark sense of humour and vulnerability, plus a way of "brazenly embracing anger, absurdity, complexity, the whole shebang." That's got to be close. Meanwhile I'd say you've already spent too much time hanging out in the kitchen overhearing second-hand descriptions when you could be out there imbibing the dangerous stuff itself. So get going.

Don McKay

Salmon River Motel

Between dry eyes of the Shuswap
a dog-day migraine pounds as high pressure goads air
into something it can't take back,
some criminal friction with sun. Neither gives,
chest to swelling chest, lording it
as the Houseboat Capital of Canada squirms and sours.
A mountain south of the Number 1
begins to burn. Nothing to do with me.
Driving west, merely night blind, I take a room
as evening starts to run its phantom deer across the road.

This is how I remember desire:
all heat and bad timing. Red sinking sun,
brief period of blindness. The panicky swerve
from nothing to nowhere
that takes your face in its hands and screams it's time
to shut the engine down.

Hell has gone guerrilla in the hills,
slipping its threats under doors. I've run out of towels.
My air conditioner is cranked and coughing.
There's a small fridge for beer.
Across the street at A-1 Taxidermy two men work
to spare their dead a decent burial of fire.
Lions lie with lambs in the rusted box of a half-ton,
a furry *Guernica*.
I watch this on TV, having removed my shoes.
Only reporters are happy, changing and changing their shirts.

The town is evacuating, air thick with the terror of elk,
and I'm thinking of a man pushing a mower endlessly
along the perimeter of a seaside lawn,
how he filled my lungs with something heavier than breath.
Of the woman who calls him in to supper.
Does this make me a villain?
If I can't sleep then no one here will sleep.
It's important to stay in character. Meanwhile

Karen Solie

firefighters converge as though more noble aspects
could be differentiated and made flesh.
They consume food and sleep with a purity learned
from how fire takes unto itself the perfumes
of a forest's private lives and spirals with them
in rapture above the canopy. Tending backburn,
their bodies are as fervent
doing exactly what they should and where.
Finding those hot spots. Digging them out.
It's easy to forget they are paid.

Tomorrow I'll make a run
up the corporate limit's eastern slope above
the lake hanging cold arms helpless as a bruise,
radio advising those who must leave animals
to free them, that they will gather
on the shore and be saved.
Something to tell the children.
Fiddling the dial, water bombers no bigger than flies,
I'll be gunning for the salt heart of the Island, absolved
by virtue of passing through.

Driving Alone

You learn the names given to light,
the visual heft
of a boreal forest at noon, or evening
performing by heart its declension
above the flatlands,
at the expense of your own
small word for yourself: a fence
that needs mending.
The unreadable sign. In the language
of local economies you are table 12.
room 105. Pure transaction.
A sure thing of money changing hands.

At night, scenery and time are nouns
you drive through,
double lane anodyne of wind and tires,
unable to lift your eyes from road to stars
as might a passenger
who in describing their patterns
would offer adjectives like a hand
around yours in the dark.
How beautiful. Yes.
A way of naming everything at once,
this memory made in a marriage
between you.

Karen Solie

Design Flaw

The city settles into its grid and gears,
repeats through a mouthful of wheels the distance
from my house to yours. Between them,
men and women are trying to be happy
and it's working, a beautiful machine of a day,
bees idling smoothly in the plums and children steered
along the seawall, sun a sound motor.
I lie on my back like a wrench, like the wrong tool
for the job or an error in judgment,
considering our contraption, its constant backfiring
and exposed wires. The bad shocks.
Tricky choke. Our wild rides
among heat and oils of internal combustion.
The volatility of bones.

In Praise of Grief

Come home from a day
in the world and it talks
you down;
there's always something
you should know, some small way
you're fooling yourself.
There are people
who live whole lives coddled
as eggs.
You're blessed.

Night vision glasses, articulate
nurse, it lays
barbiturate fingers on your brow,
undresses you slowly
and stays,
holds your hand until
you sleep, mouth watering.
It's that sweet, nesting
in the cairn of your chest. In fact,
a kind of beauty, showing
what is not in everything
that is; and all
it wants to talk about
is you.

Helen Tsiriotakis is a poet of a renewed and complex lyricism. Her first book, A *House of White Rooms*, is a long poem composed of free-standing poems and sections in prose, with Mnemosyne, the figure of memory, the mother of muses, as the centering if not central presence. The poet, who knows intimately the Greece of today as well as its cultural memory, locates in myth and history and personal experience a new sense of song. The poems selected for inclusion in this anthology, by strategies of naming, accomplish lyric intensity within a large structure.

The most violently lyric of Helen Tsiriotakis' poems are often without the lyric "I." The I turns into—translates as—you, she, they. Or even as skin, as a house. The shape-shifting I flashes, dances, shimmers, teases, disappears, as language locates and dissolves possible identities. The name of the game is not being but rather desiring.

These poems of memory are about remembering forward. The I is unable to find or even assume a stable existence. This is not a poetry of repose. The voices remember in the present tense. What is past is future, what is future is already past; the point of speaking is where we locate ourselves as readers. We listen for glimpses of the visible.

In these poems, movement and energy challenge the conventional notion of knowledge. We as readers must allow ourselves equal riskiness, even a counter-memory, a dislocation.

Robert Kroetsch

Mnemosyne

I

A flush of stardust
as night drains from horizons.

The moulting earth is a new expression
relumed in its nakedness, its
liquid fire, full
of roused season, waiting
to be born.

.

In Nitros, inhibitions are unhinged
and light slides into place like a bolt.

Knuckles of hills implode into valleys.
Our calloused skin
impaled, secreting time's geography.
An evolution of vapours. Everything whispered
and gliding.

Teased through edges
purls of dust roil the river's shallows: what they dance

is what they've heard.

II

Her web of leaves over wind-burned fields
ignites the gauze of autumn.

November. Cold night.
Mnemosyne wanders the foothills,
polished moonlight
dangles from wrists and ankles,
braided hair beating
in muffled chords.

Here, under a clotting dusk,
sleeping vines insinuate
festivals of wine—
where rainy nights, simmering
dishes of pearl-white rice in grape leaves,
dip into lemon broth
and stir a seduction.
Star-drenched nights. The waning.

Mnemosyne lingers a glance
to earth, to water, as if looking to drag in
the one she's losing. The perforated air
licked by her tongue of sparks.

She says nothing. Instead,
as she raises bare hands
her bones rattle their burden: crossed arms
binding stooped shoulders:
the baggage she carries.

Her fear the same as her desire:
in name only
ticking the other direction.

With nowhere to hide.

Shadow Hand

Another girl who presents herself as a memory.
One more shape of memory.

The girl approaches a wall, casting a shadow. With chalk she traces her own image, diving down the cliff neck, climbing a hill shoulder, following the length of a long torso. To maintain the shape, she knows she must keep still. She must also keep the distance. If she pinpoints the light, chalkdust draws out her obscurity, radiating messy confessions: under prescriptive scrutiny, she blurs the look of the lens. When she's too far, lifelines withdraw. She associates with the tip of any diversion. She stands this way for hours, outlining the memory of her body. Until she reaches the part of the wall where her hand collides with the shadow's hand. No matter the impression she leaves, she confronts her own solitude. Her chalk can't embody the hand that holds it. This is her alternate route: placing the chalk in her left hand, her right hand leaning against the wall.

Her right hand leaning against the wall.

Constantly Stirring

An old woman peers into a mailbox;
her hope squints round an invisible letter.

Hers are the children of a migrant generation.
From a room in a house on the hilltops of Crete
she blends the kindred appetites.
Crickets clamour
their treetop table,
as if banging lids of pans, and the panting wind
like an exhausted messenger
pitches basil bouquets through her open window.

The olive groves my father planted as a child:
a sprouting hunger
yearning the sprawling field.
While roots cross like an old man's legs.
I don't know him in this posture.
This waiting that consents.

Hunger carved out my mother's second language
pronouncing *psomi* as bread.
Cutting her in half, one part
caught in the motive that held the blade, the other
the size of the border she was crossing.

It's an ocean that keeps my parents' past
in every house but ours:

Blood bleached with experience
resembles water.

Soon I'll watch the old woman blend
immiscible circumstance,
olive oil and water. In this stone-floor kitchen.
In a deepening bowl. Wondering how much
is too much. How much is enough.
How else to reunite

the child whose prying fingers
once churned soil to blossoms
with the child whose choices
unfurled a new flag. How to reconcile
boundaries, as heat
from land where your dead are remembered
kindles another country's womb—
And weakening doubts diffuse as if wind.

                                          Believe the grain
of a second language, chafing conversations,
keeps us listening; all sight is sculpted
by gradations of light. As we bridge continents.
The distance between
where you are
and what you love:
a handspan.

An old woman constantly stirring.

From an emulsion of olive oil and water
she whisks landscapes. Sifting flour.

Honey-glazed cakes rising.
Emerging guests to a cluttered occasion.

Helen Tsiriotakis

I first met Sheila Waite in 1991. She was a student in one of my writing classes at the University of Toronto. She was writing stories then. Her prose was suspenseful, lithe, alert. She seemed to understand instinctively that lyricism is not flabby (the most common misapprehension) but, on the contrary, the leanest line there is; not skin and bone, but muscle. It was clear that she also understood the necessity of apprenticeship; that the best writing takes years of dedicated effort—among other things, to learn technique, to "develop one's voice," to wrestle down the various demons that can sabotage even a strong gift. To negotiate the relationship between creative surrender and authorial control. As part of this apprenticeship—taking on what she felt was the most difficult form—Sheila started to work on poems. After several years she wrote a "breakthrough" poem: fully-realized, taut and deep, a poem called "Animals Dream." This was to become the core of a manuscript called *Earth Wife*. These are Sheila's comments:

> "...Worked five years on a book of poetry which began after a trip to Malaysia. Research on the archipelago led to discovering families of pirates in the Arabian Sea, and powerful women [Such as Nur Jahan] in Mughal India. The centerpiece of the book is a poem ["Animals Dream"] about transformation, rooted in mythology. *Earth Wife*, like all good journeys, is about becoming intimate with the world. The exotic fascinates and frightens.

Colours are hidden behind screens. Longing.
In a new land, the self is revealed. Boundaries
are broken and restored…"

Sheila was born in 1947, and grew up in Port Credit, Ontario. For the past fifteen years, she has taught at the Ontario College of Art and Design. It is entirely characteristic that she is now tackling a new form; I've read some scenes from the play she's working on, and they are vivid, original, energized with intent. Over the course of a decade, I've witnessed Sheila's integrity; she works with diligence and humility. Two lines of her poetry represent both her poems and her process: "Shame is shed in the forgiving ground" and—it gives me pleasure to quote this—"alive as magenta."

Anne Michaels

Black Rushes

Queen of the Nile,
let me be your boat the thousand miles.

Let me spin a cocoon of caresses
where we can hide.

I walk in your footsteps,
hearing you, never finding you.

I collect moments for you,
the wind washes them to desert lands.
I imagine our sea-horse bodies
touching for the first time.

Strong oars, or a pillow of stars.

*   *

In dreams, our love is paradise,
golden days fade to silver.

Save me,
angel.

*   *

And then I see you
like the dead arisen,
wearing the fragile dress
that haunts me.

You are perfection,
it destroys me to love you.

Swan on a black pond.
Now I'm waiting
just to drown.

Sheila Waite

Wide White Bed

('Thaipusam', Hindu holy day of repentance)

Between earth and heaven
blossoms live on air and atoms.
Jewels hatched from teeming decay.

*   *

At Batu caves, throngs of pilgrims swallowing dust,
rivers of monks flowing in saffron and
girls from plantations alive as magenta
climb three hundred steps
for 'Thaipusam'.

A woman wrapped in white
rolls down the temple stairway,
ripe, delicate in muslin.
Enraptured, I watch the humble act
weightless as stone in orbit.
Long to inhabit the small island
between her outstretched hands, bare toes.
Her family spreads a path of magnolia
as she empties
into a violet beginning.
Eyelids, coal hair shivering.

I lose her as she disperses,
yet his Love contains her.

*   *

Spikes mortify cheeks
smeared with ash.
Bones melt in ecstasy.
In torsos of believers, lattices
heavy with feathers and fruit,
hang from hooks.

Following the scent of salvation
they move up and up.

Towards the dark cave
lit by fire and hope.

      *   *

In Singapore on a wide white bed
suddenly we are two countries—
our interlude, a year of blue
letters and continents drifting between.
Now silence, dense as teakwood.
In my animal eye
streets swim black and oily,
swarms of hostile faces,
I slip to the bottom of the world,
the small place in me drowns.
Will I be your wife?

      *   *

Do not wander alone
into the womb of the first hot ferns.
Lose me in valleys breathing smoke through your land.
Our green / crimson blood,
have I told you how I need you?
I swim upstream into your mystery.
Flash of teeth, soaked skin,
willingly, I enter your fantasy.

In the cave, on the temple stairs,
the surrender of raw souls.
Are there flowers for our road?

      *   *

A coconut dashed to the earth,
the priest touches the burning spot.
From praying palms
devotion evaporates towards god.
Shame is shed into the forgiving ground.

Feel closer, the next day
in the bleached street,
looking for curry.

You teach me degrees of heat.

Sheila Waite

Song of the Sea and You

I lose you, your face
as your ship carries you further
from shore.

Your voice, once
breath warming my skin,
in howling winds
drowns.

At night, our bed rocks,
waves roar in my ears.
Cracks in the dirt floor
fill with my tears.

My body is pulled
to the land's strong curves—
to emerald hills with
yellow flames of corn.
Limb and root
restore me.

Gazing upon the sea,
the vastness blinds me.
I wait for you to return
from the world's end.

C*arousel* came to me as a gift, the first I knew of GEORGE WHIPPLE. One read-through put me in search of the two others. All I have gleaned about the writer is from dust jackets: He has lived in New Brunswick, Toronto, and is now in or near Vancouver. His current photograph *looks* young (to me)—but in 1996 he wrote, "I'm old. / I can't compete / with who I was." Still, three years later *Carousel* proves that he could! His work is inerrant in touch, awaking a reader, to see and feel truth. The words are simple but evoke space and life, extraordinarily—

Let the books speak: of the way breaking waves "unweave in the freshet foam"; how "Flowers love the snow / although it kills them—roses / wrapped in luscious tissue-paper shrouds"; and a cow's "drooling mushroom muzzle". In "Poem Poem", Whipple hints how poems can "decriminalize the senses", offering a line-drawing, opposite, of a hieratic, faintly mocking insect. Is this man a farmer? or an entymologist—see his fly's "humungous-huge orbed head"? or a musician—as "Music" or "Wednesday Morning Blues" suggest? Or an artist? All through *Carousel* the drawings, on facing pages, keep communicating with the poems.

He knows, too, what to say—or rather how to keep the silence—"Down / at the wounded / doorway of the soul…"

Margaret Avison

Music

Fingers float
    over strings, A dance
of body language; hands
and arms moving in unison,
    heads bobbing up and down
as in a trance.

The longer one listens
    the shorter the distance
seems between death and birth,
we are part of all that is and never was
as clouds that pass from one life
    to another in a breath.

Lunar blue
    the low-pitched oboe breathes,
illuminates landscapes of sorrow,
almost explains the death of children;
    on the outskirts of hearing
    a door is opened to knowledge
beyond all other knowing.

All things disappear in time,
    yet in the amber of eternity are kept
    as the saffron light of summer
    in the eerie timbre of a clarinet,
darkness in the shadow of violas.

George Whipple

Christmas Eve

Down
at the wounded
doorway of the soul
where all men jackknife, break,
and are remade with pleasure
in Time's cave
(machined by Eve
rotating with clasped Mars),
bent-kneed through straw,
his hands like stars,
the wordless, wet
incarnate Word
appears.

A Hymn To God The Father

O God invisible as music, let me know
Thee in the least reflection of Thy much,
in termite, tick and earwig, in the glow-
worm striking matches on the dark, the house-
fly scratching his humungous-huge orbed head;
in all the creepy, crawly, earthbound things;
the bandy ant in black fatigues, the slow
gelatinous, fat snail.
                      Although I climb
to Thee in prayers that fall as if unsaid,
O Alpha and Omega, Logos, great I AM,
I know Thee in the nit, mosquito, flea;
in pollywog, boll weevil, gnat and louse
—and with the praying mantis, worship Thee.

George Whipple

Prospectus

Plonger au fond du gouffre...
                       Baudelaire

The dead. Explore the look they have—they know
between two lives the greatest distance is a breath.
Beyond all pain they live, apothecary souls
without our hinged appliances of flesh
and bone. On soles of air, resilient
as the wind, they float
in an eternal now.
More delicate than candle smoke they glide
down corridors invisible, of branching faiths,
into bright riverview apartments pre-prepared
by that most courteous of consorts, death.

*

Innocent, the sea collects the sturgeon's milt:
the small moist wounds re-open, start to ooze
mucilaginous cool eggs. From viscid roots
flowers rise: protruding through the snow
they spring into bouquets for lovers mock
time for a night before they too shall fade
au fond de l'inconnu pour trouver du nouveau.

The Anatomy Lesson

Take up your scalpels, my white coated crows.

Draw nearer as I split the ribcage, shuck
from its sheathlike pericardium
the heart. It pumped, hydraulic dynamo,
for 80 years according to his toe-tag—
until a thrombus, this pimento clot,
brought him here.

                Look closely as I
anatomize the ear's coiled cochlea;
slit the lightless porthole of the eye,
open the strategic tunnel of the throat.

Next, pass this wrinkled sponge around—the brain,
where sparks, synaptic charges in a data-dance
of stimulus/response, make up intelligence
some call the soul—but I (who sever, saw
and sheer, who study still to understand
what *can* be understood) don't lance
cadavers for what can't be seen:
the flesh is miracle enough.

                Dissect the hands
a violin drew music from; the foot
and ankle where all marathons began;
the tongue and larynx silence used for speech.
Drill the skull's domed theatre where dreams
found love and glory unattainable elsewhere...
My God! I'm waxing metaphysical or worse.

It's late, meet here after lunch.

Class dismissed.

George Whipple

Easter Egg

In the convent ear of a ravine
hushed by twenty centuries of hills
I saw the moon unwrapped from silverfoil;
saw hands that made both Easter egg and hen
crack open night's hard, brittle shell
releasing the gold sunbird sealed within:
everything around me sang with light.
The morning whispered life and death are one.

Though beauty brings us back—and back
from life beyond the train,
from speeding windows now and then
we see another world awaiting our arrival.

What earth's not trenched with graves,
not laced with shattered seed the sun revives?

CARLETON WILSON is already a leader in the group of young poets who wed intelligence and fresh feeling to a renewed concern for poetic form. His is an earthen voice, tanging of clay, bark and iron, of rain or dusk light on rails, gleaming sidewalks, concrete walls. Its richness comes from its own depths, though, not from gritty subject matter, for it also can speak with a touch of Laforgue's irony about graceful or fantastic things. Wilson relates that he "plucked the blunt bone from its muddy pit" and saw in a badger's skull "the conceptions / of scrounge and scurry were left in the form / of packed dirt". Exchanging the subterranean and theroid for the supernal, he also describes angels who struck Rumi to the ground with a revelation: "collapsing his height / by unknown feats of spiritual engineering, each / celestial frame then retreated into a sheen / of sunlight".

Eloquence exactly fitted like this to its meaning is rare. Wilson's fine verbal imagination blends the aulic and the colloquial and finds (or makes up) surprising words to create many a memorable line: "the underscore of strewn chestnuts / I kicked at as I walked along", "the stunted phrasing of boxcar wheels", the moon "holding sway over the dank mask in my hand". He reverences the traditions of poetry. His sonnets, for example, renovate the ancient genre with novel rhythms and many finely invented assonances, consonances, off-rhymes, hypermetrical rhymes and the like. Look at the subtle, expressive pattern of the syllables ending with "r" in the last three lines of "Junction Sonnets I" (ear, air, pure, are, bear, their) and at the counterpoint played in the first of these lines by syllables with "r" at their start (drum, brisk, cross). Everywhere in Wilson's verse, mastery carries thought and emotion quietly into the heart.

A.F. Moritz

Intelligent Crockery

> When the badger glimmered away
> into another garden
> you stood, half-lit with whiskey,
> sensing you had disturbed
> some soft returning.
> —Seamus Heaney

Digging into the backyard earth with a sod shovel,
turning the vernal garden this evening
with the twilit sky balanced between night and day,
the eclipse of the spring equinox,
I hit bone. The sound was a dull thud in my ears.
As I burrowed down about the bony revelation,
I cast a glance upwards at the sky darkening
with each blink into a deeper blue than before,
then bent and reached with fingers outstretched
and plucked the blunt bone from its muddy pit.
The skull of a badger. It was heavier than I first
thought, heavier probably than at the initial
moment of its last impression.

Inside this bone bowl that once possessed
weasel-genius, the remnants of the conceptions
of scrounge and scurry were left in the form
of packed dirt, the elements of the badger's
transgressions made manifest within the place
they first originated. My grip tightened around
the numbing object, my thumb in one of the eye sockets,
rubbing the orbital arc as if to conjure the creature-soul
from shrivelled matter. Lifting it close
to my face, I peered deeply into the space just
before the bone, realised black fur surrounding
even blacker eyes, blinking void back at me.

Carleton Wilson

The moon rising moved across the sky from east
to west, holding sway over the dank mask in my hand.
A tidal bone whose orbit about my own head
was manipulated with the passing of each
moment, its ultimate end
all arc weld and grafting—
fusion within a human skull.

Moonfall and the sky blackened to pitch,
revealing the universe to a glance,
the only light a shadow of itself.
I will just lie here in the cool grass
with the smell of freshly dug earth
rooted in my head
and feel fiendish for a while, be a badger.

At Dusk

Twilight, & you shrink from it, folding yourself
into a tightly knit wool sweater. Yet only
concrete walls hide you enough to lift your head
from the crook of your elbow, a young lamb
losing herself, quiet with the presence of wolves.

An *umbrella,*

fluttering patterns,
folded but
unstrapped,

propped
in the corner
or

hanging on
a wooden hook
in the hallway,

still dripping
from your early
morning stroll

down quiet junction
lanes, red cobbled
brick giving way

in jagged patterns
to the dappled
gray of pavement,

like ice melting
at the edge of
a spring river,

might recall the
rain-wetted afternoon
we met

last autumn,
leaves tumbling
down about us,

if only I hadn't
decided to stay
home that day.

Carleton Wilson

Rumi

I imagined it as a kind of pulley & lever system,
   lowering the stunned Rumi to the ground,
a road crew of worker-angels sweating in the late
   morning heat, coughing from effort, the air
thick with dust. Laying him out onto the packed
   dirt of the roadway, collapsing his height
by unknown feats of spiritual engineering, each
   celestial frame then retreated into a sheen
of sunlight, leaving only Rumi's prostrate form,
   unconscious of anything at all but the one
question that caused him to fall to the hard earth.

And standing slightly off to the side, Shams was
   smiling, eyes dancing a mad dervish in the
sockets of his skull. He'd long been searching for one
   like this, had offered his head as sacrifice
for the holy pleasure of such pure conversation. And
   so here, on the road leading into Konya,
Shams' wanderings were wholly rewarded with this
   sputtering, speechless form at his feet. As
Rumi struggled up from the vast depths of voice &
   meaning into which he'd fallen, Shams knew
this was only the first of many answers to come.

from Junction Sonnets

I

Light fragmented and trestlework shadows
upon the ground: the walking bridge a black
iron diphthong rising above steel rails.
Underneath, gleaming silver, the train tracks
curve northwest through factory landscape,
liquid like mercury in thin autumn light.
From above—my shadow sliding across this faded
strip of field, a whisper of me—I hear the bright,

sibilant hiss of wind through yellowed grass
below, and the stunted phrasing of boxcar wheels
crossing a branching track is a distant tap on the
ear-drum. In this brisk air these pure and dross
sounds are a patchwork of syllable and speech
that bear me inside their language and beyond it.

II

Chestnuts scatter the ground: their prickly green
husks and deep brown hearts punctuate the dull
noise of the concrete, accent fallen leaves
on a softly murmuring lawn. In the quiet lull
of childhood I first happened upon this postcard—
this autumn scene underwrit and whispered in
my ear. On that walk to school early in October
I don't remember the dark tree that must've been

there, only the underscore of strewn chestnuts
I kicked at as I walked along. But the picture
is more complete now: trunk and canopy
rise and spread above like widening vistas;
subtle subtext causes each colour and texture
to fall from its secret place and speak to me.

Carleton Wilson

Marilyn Bowering
   Human Bodies, New and Selected Poems 1987-1999, Beach Holme, 1999
   Visible Worlds, HarperCollins, 1997
   Autobiography, Beach Holme, 1996
   To All Appearances a Lady, Random House Canada, 1989
   Calling All the World, Laika and Fochakov 1957, Press Porcepic, 1989

James Clarke
   The Way Everyone Is Inside, Exile Editions, 2000
   The Ancient Pedigree of Plums, Exile Editions, 1999
   The Raggedy Parade, Exile Editions, 1998
   Silver Mercies, Exile Editions, 1997
   Globe & Mail, "Facts & Arguments," July 16th, 1998

Carla Funk
   Blessing the Bones into Light, Coteau Books, 1999
   Hammers & Tongs: A Smoking Lung Anthology, Smoking Lung Press, 1999
   Solomon's Wives (chapbook), Smoking Lung Press, 1997
   Breathing Fire, Harbour Publishing, 1995
   Inner Harbour Review, Vol. 1, University of Victoria, 1994

Susan Holbrook
   Dandelion, Summer 2000
   misled, Red Deer Press, 1999
   Hot & Bothered II, Arsenal Pulp Press, 1999
   Fireweed, No. 62, Summer 1998
   The Capilano Review, Vol. 2, No. 16, 1995

Suzette Mayr
   Prairie Fire, Vol. 20, No. 3, Fall 1999
   The Widows, NeWest Press, 1998
   Moon Honey, NeWest Press, 1995
   Zebra Talk (chapbook), disOrientation Press, 1991

rob mclennan
   side/lines: a poetic, Insomniac Press, 2001
   harvest: a book of signifiers, Talonbooks, 2001
   bagne, or Criteria for Heaven, Broken Jaw Press, 2000
   Shadowy Technicians: New Ottawa Poets, Broken Jaw Press, 2000
   The Richard Brautigan Ahhhhhhhhhhh, Talonbooks, 1999

George Murray
   The Cottage Builder's Letter, McClelland & Stewart, 2001
   Carousel: A Book of Second Thoughts, Exile Editions, 2000
   Descant, No. 111, Winter 2000
   Prairie Fire, Vol. 21, No. 3, Fall 2000
   Ontario Review, No. 53

Selected Publications

Elizabeth Philips
   Prairie Fire, Vol. 21, No. 2, Summer 2000
   A Blue with Blood in it, Coteau Books, 2000
   The Malahat Review, No. 125, Spring 1998
   Beyond My Keeping, Coteau Books, 1995
   Time in a Green Country, Coteau Books, 1990

Karen Solie
   Short Haul Engine, Brick Books, 2001
   Malahat Review, No. 132, Fall 2000
   Fiddlehead, No. 204, Summer 2000
   Event, Vol. 28, No. 2, Summer 1999
   Arc, No. 42, Summer 1999

Helen Tsiriotakis
   A House of White Rooms, Coach House Books, 2000
   Queen Street Quarterly, Vo. 2, No. 3, Fall 1998
   Quarry, Vol. 42, No.4, 1994

Sheila Waite
   Unpublished.

George Whipple
   Tom Thomson & Other Poems, Penumbra Press, 2000
   Carousel, Ekstasis Press, 1999
   Hats Off to the Sun, Ekstasis Press, 1996
   Passing Through Eden, Thistledown Press, 1991
   Life Cycle, Hounslow Press, 1984

Carleton Wilson
   Hart House Review, Spring 2000
   The Fiddlehead, No. 202, Winter 2000
   Intelligent Crockery/Ominous Wicker Stuff (chapbook), Junction Books, 2000
   Junction Sonnets (chapbook), Junction Books, 1999
   Queen Street Quarterly, Vol. 3, No. 3, Fall 1999